A VIRTUOUS CYCLE

A VIRTUOUS CYCLE

Living in Abundance through the Cycle of Charity, Relevance, and Influence

BENJAMIN GENET

CERTIFIED

(H)

WRITTEN
BY HUMAN

CONTENTS

FOREWORD

By Rabbi Dr. Kenneth Brander

In "A Virtuous Cycle," Ben J. Genet shares his insights on how giving charity can improve our satisfaction with all aspects of our lives, as well as help boost our personal and financial success. Generosity leads to renewed appreciation of everything from our families to our professional accomplishments, ultimately creating momentum in all that we do.

Through clear and concise writing, this easy-to-read book teaches us how to start giving more and building that momentum in our lives. At the heart of the book's message is learning to look at life through the prism of abundance instead of scarcity

Through examples and stories, including those from Jewish sources and tradition, he shows us how to lead life in a manner that helps us switch our outlook from scarcity to abundance. This is a paradigm switch that can improve marriages, family interactions, businesses—essentially every part of our lives while simultaneously improving the society around us.

The shift from a mindset of scarcity to abundance is not limited to money. Genet also shares through personal examples how giving time and attention to people or projects is another form of generosity that leads to improvement and success. This wider focus on generosity makes this a book that can improve our lives whether our financial contributions are large or small, and guide as we grow and our lives become more expansive.

He introduces concepts that show us how to stay relevant and purposeful – how to constantly improve ourselves while helping to change the world. This leads to greater wealth and increased relevance in this world. Whether by giving funds or expertise, giving to others can help all of us gain influence and make a difference in our daily lives, both personal and financial.

This is a book that is not only appropriate for business people and entrepreneurs, but also for clergy members, communal professionals, and heads of nonprofits. It creates a new context to both giving and soliciting support. Reading this book will inspire you and leave you open to the challenge of making your life better and more meaningful.

In fact, you will likely ask yourself why you didn't embrace such logical and sensible-sounding ideas before reading this book. Sometimes the best books are the ones that just help you frame ideas that you always knew to be purposeful and prudent – enjoy the book.

PREFACE

The world has changed.

I began writing this book before October 7th, 2023. On that day, the terror group Hamas brutally attacked Israel, killing over 1,300 and kidnapping at least 130 more. Much has been said about the attack since.

In the weeks following the attack, my wife and I traveled to Israel to help in whatever way was needed. We gave money–a topic I cover throughout this book–and we gave time and energy. As Israeli men and women were mobilized into the army, the need for replacement labor was immediate. We helped where we could.

We also sat with family members who had lost loved ones in the attack and whose loved ones were kidnapped and being held by the terrorists. What would you do? What would you ask of others in that situation?

This is a book about giving, and the immense joy and tangible benefits I have received as a result of my lifelong practice of giving money to causes I believe are important.

The attacks of October 7th have not increased the need for generosity in the world–the need is always there and the need is great–but they have grabbed us by the collar and forced us to confront the need in a new way.

My hope is that you invest a couple of hours to read this book– that's all it will require. Then, I pray that you take the lessons I have learned about generosity and use them in your own life, in your own way.

Do it because it's the right and moral thing to do, or do it because you will receive real benefit from giving. Regardless of your motivation, the person you help is helped.

Before October 7th, this book was solely focused on the value of giving money to charity. Since October 7th, I've learned the value of giving time and attention to people.

Sitting with a family member of one of the Israeli hostages held in Gaza in the days after the attack, I learned that my mere presence and attention were a gift that brought real benefit to that family member.

INTRODUCTION

For most of my life, I was living in a scarcity mindset.

Whether in business, finances, or personal relationships, I held the false belief that the goal was to take as much as I could get–and squeeze it tightly in my fist so no one else could take it from me.

I began to change little by little. By 2018, the results of my changes kicked in, and my life transformed.

My business portfolio doubled. The phone rang off the hook with people wanting to do business with me. My existing relationships grew richer, and my life was blessed with new friendships with people who share my values. My employees loved working with me. I became well-known in my community; if I wanted something, people listened. I found myself having incredible experiences that I thought I'd never have: traveling the world to make an impact, being honored for my positive contributions, and, most importantly, being proud of myself.

Most importantly, I felt so much better on the inside because I learned how to live in abundance. I stopped squeezing my fist and instead opened my palm to share my blessings with others. As a result, the love and joy in my life grew exponentially.

What changed?

For years, I had given to charity, but suddenly, all of that giving began flooding back to me…and I was able to give on a level I'd never imagined before.

I had always tithed, even when I was young and not yet financially successful, but this was different. Tithing is like paying a tax or a bill—you give away a percentage of your earnings because you know you have to. Tithing is important, but what I'm talking about in this book is much bigger… It's a way to reframe the focus of your life so that your financial success benefits others, not only yourself. I'm talking about giving away amounts that other people might find ridiculous…

This book is written for entrepreneurs and people who have attained some wealth. It's also aimed at young clergy and communal professionals. Entrepreneurs have the freedom to change their futures based on how they see the world. While anyone can and should give to charity, this book specifically discusses how entrepreneurs can leverage their wealth by giving to charity and impacting the world.

As a business owner, I've now reached the point where the money my business makes doesn't go to making my lifestyle more extravagant. Instead, I've turned my business into a machine for earning money for *others*. I make deals so I can earn more money to give away. To most business owners, this sounds crazy... But I will show you how doing this transformed every facet of my life.

This book is a continuation of my last book, *Born Jumping*. If you've read the book, you'll remember the Jumper Success Formula: discipline, focus, and intention. You need all three of these things to get anywhere in life. But in this book, I'm going to take the formula a step further and show you how to apply it to making an impact on the world.

See, we could apply this formula to business or making money all we want, but if we fail to connect it to our purpose or causes we're passionate about, our success can still be empty. This book is for people who have achieved success and now want to learn how to use their success to do good and live out their values. On the flip side, pursuing charity without discipline, focus, or intention won't work either.

What if we treated charity like we treat running a business? When you're running a business, all that matters at the end of the day is the bottom line. Did you profit or not? It doesn't matter how hard you work, how much time you put in, or how good you feel. It's about the result. I believe we should view charity in the same way. It's not about how many hours you volunteered or how hard you worked to organize a benefit event. Doing these things makes you feel good, but how many people's lives did you impact? Did it make a sufficient impact?

The end result is the only metric I use in my quest to improve the lives of others.

It's my mission to tell the world about the unbelievable transformation that happens in your life when you commit to giving. If you don't give, you miss out on these opportunities.

Personally, I plan to give away half of my net worth in my lifetime. When I die, 30% of my estate will go to charity, and last year, I gave $1.85 million to causes I believe in.

I don't say all this to brag—I say it to show you what could be possible.

Since I began giving to charity, my business has been more successful, I've made more money, and my net worth has grown exponentially. My wife loves me more, I have better friends, and my employees respect me.

Since I began giving to charity, my business has been more successful, I've made more money, and my net worth has grown exponentially. My wife loves me more, I have better friends, and my employees respect me. I've become well-known in my community, and I've gained influence that allows me to help others and accomplish their goals in ways that I would never have thought possible before. I have my name on buildings, I've been given honorary degrees, and I've had auditoriums full of people celebrating my contributions...and I am happier with who I am and how I show up in the world.

Most importantly, the insecurity I struggled with as a young man continues diminishing, and I'm happier than ever.

Every facet of my life has become more abundant, and I have more love and joy in my life.

But let me make an important distinction: I don't give to charity to get these benefits. I give to charity because it's the right thing to do, and it's satisfying to help others. I feel no shame about enjoying the benefits that come back to me when I give to charity, and I think it's important to tell others that you can expect the same benefits when you give. A deeply altruistic person might not care about the benefits they receive from doing good, but most of us aren't like that.

> The word "charity" is limited. It's defined by Merriam-Webster as "generosity and helpfulness, especially toward the needy or suffering." The Hebrew word *tzedaka* which means "righteousness," describes an obligation. It's more about the givers' engagement in making the world a better place.

The word "philanthropy" captures this higher intent: "goodwill to fellow members of the human race, especially: active effort to promote human welfare; or an act or gift done or made for humanitarian purposes."

I don't give to charity so I can get these benefits.
I give to charity because it's the right thing to do, and it's satisfying to help others.

I also feel no guilt about pursuing wealth. I believe that if you can attain wealth, it's a noble effort to grow your wealth so you can share it with those in need. As your wealth grows, your ability to impact the world grows, too. No giving can happen if you can't afford to give. So, I would argue that focusing on the benefits you receive, your business, and your success can be a holy endeavor if you use some of those proceeds to help others.

In this book, I will share the path to enriching your life through charity...the path that I walked which led me to an ever-improving and amazing life, despite my many struggles, that I never knew could be within my reach.

Abundance, contribution, and wealth are a cycle

Before you can give, you need to have abundance. This doesn't necessarily mean wealth—you need to have an abundance mindset, not a scarcity mindset. Abundance means having a positive outlook and believing there will always be more.

More money, more opportunities, more love…

When you have a scarcity mindset, you want to hold tightly to what you have and compete with others for it because you believe there's not enough to go around.

If you have a fist full of sand and squeeze it tightly to keep as much of the sand as you can, it'll fall through the cracks. That's a scarcity mindset. "More for me, less for you." When you have an abundance mindset, you hold the sand with an open palm. You know that if sand falls out of your hand, it's okay because you can always pick up more.

When you have abundance, you can contribute. Someone who's broke or living paycheck-to-paycheck isn't able to contribute to charity. They need to pinch their pennies to cover their own needs. But when you have abundant money, you have more than enough to cover your needs. You can contribute some of your wealth to charity.

And when you contribute your wealth, wealth comes back to you. Whether it's monetary wealth, a wealth of relationships, or a wealth of influence, your business will do better because charity will strengthen your reputation in the community. The effect of that reputation is more opportunity.

Giving enhances reputation, and a great reputation is a magnet for opportunity.

You'll be able to build new relationships with like-minded people, which will open your life to so many new ideas and opportunities. And you'll gain influence... It turns out that when you can write a big check, people are willing to listen to what you say. Suddenly, you can become a powerful advocate for causes that are important to you and influence others to make decisions that align with your charitable goals. Simultaneously, that will lead to better relationships and more opportunities. The circles keep spinning and growing.

This is a fundamental truth: reputation is power. When a banker is discussing whether they will give you a loan and you have a great reputation, you will likely get the loan. I pay lower interest rates than many of my competitors because I am viewed as a much safer borrower. That has to do with how I've conducted myself my entire life. Giving to charity is a big part of that because it reveals a person's character... And it sells.

People who pose as givers but don't actually give much are eventually found out. I've seen a few people continue to switch charity boards after the rest of the board finds out they aren't giving any money... Their reputation will follow them everywhere they go.

People make a show of wealth–they drive fancy cars and wear expensive jewelry and designer clothing–but for some reason, they refuse to brag about their charity.
It should be the opposite.

But if you build a strong reputation through charitable giving, you'll find it easier to get your way.

And it's not a one-and-done deal. It's a cycle that will get bigger and better throughout your life. You give to charity and reap the benefits. These benefits give you a greater ability to give to charity, so the next year, you give more... As a result of giving more, you get bigger and better benefits. Your giving grows, and amazing things happen. Soon, you find that you're able to have an impact on the world and change people's lives.

In an interview, successful tech investor Naval Ravikant shared his belief that "All returns in life come from compound interest." Meaning, the length and strength of your commitments over time yield rewards. When you invest money, the longer that investment compounds, the greater your eventual reward will be. When you're married, the longer you maintain a relationship with your spouse, the deeper and happier that relationship will be. It's the same with any relationship, whether it's with a business partner or a friend—time invested compounds and leads to greater rewards in the future. And as an entrepreneur, you likely already know that the value of your business compounds over time as the seeds you planted years ago grow and bear fruit.

In life, great rewards come to those who play the long game, not those who over-optimize for the moment.

It works the same with charity... The impact of your contribution will compound over time both in your community, with the charities you support, and with your personal and business relationships. It will bring increased goodness to every area of your life. This impact may not feel like much in the first few years you commit to giving to charity, but it will pay huge dividends down the road.

In the rest of this book, I will share how all of this is possible.

CHAPTER 1

The Abundance Mindset

"If you want love and abundance in your life, give it away."

– Mark Twain

In the introduction, I showed you the abundance, contribution, and wealth cycle.

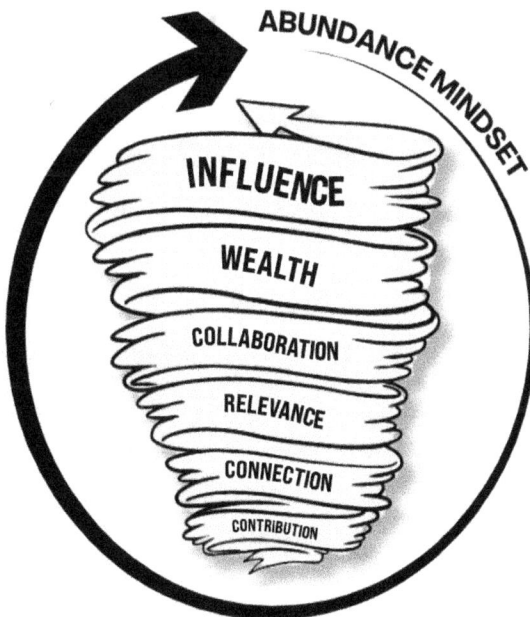

ABUNDANCE MINDSET

INFLUENCE

WEALTH

COLLABORATION

RELEVANCE

CONNECTION

CONTRIBUTION

As you move this cycle, one thing leads to another, and the rewards get bigger and better. With each "loop" around this circle, you gain more abundance, a greater ability to contribute, and more wealth. The circle becomes a spiral where each loop leads you to a new level of success.

Picture a Kung Fu master making a beautiful, groovy, swirling motion. As he makes these circles, he builds momentum. Then–BAM!–he punches in a straight line. The punch has great impact, but only after he builds momentum through the swirling motions. If you're not paying attention, it looks like the punch came out of nowhere, but it wouldn't be possible to make that swift, powerful punch without creating momentum beforehand.

It's the "twenty-year overnight success." I get a call from a buddy, "I've got an amazing deal for you…" BAM! Impact! To some people, this moment looks like a stroke of luck. But it took twenty years of building momentum to make this phone call possible. I had to create abundance, make contributions, and build wealth…over and over again in ever-expanding swirling motions to create impact in this one moment.

It's like a tornado that creates big swirls in the sky and then touches down on the ground with enormous power. Then it goes back up to the sky, keeps spinning and spinning, builds more momentum, and touches down somewhere else.

Contribution and community engagement create your swirl. Over time, little circles become bigger, and your impact grows.

But before you can spiral up through this cycle, you need to let go of negativity and scarcity and adopt an abundance mindset.

Abundance doesn't just have to do with material abundance—it's not a synonym for wealth. Abundance means choosing love over negativity. Abundance means letting go of those clenched fists and terminating relationships with negative people. When I adopted an abundance mindset, I believed I could give away what I had because I trusted that I could make more. I didn't need to squeeze every last drop out of every deal. I learned to treat people better, kinder, and more generously.

Abundance means choosing love over negativity.

The opposite of abundance is scarcity. Scarcity is negative. It makes everything in life harder because you're acting from a place of fear. When I lived in a scarcity mindset, I saw everything as a competition with only one winner. I pinched pennies because I was afraid to lose what I had. I screwed people over for a dollar because I thought that I had to take what I could get and hoard it for myself. Giving is antithetical to the scarcity mindset. That scarcity mindset will and should drive people away.

The scarcity mindset could also be called the survival mindset. When you're in survival mode, it makes sense to take what's yours and ensure no one else gets their hands on it. Yet, when you're not fighting to survive, this mindset makes you act like a jerk. People won't want to deal with you. You won't be able to build long-term business relationships because you'll burn the bridge during your first transaction. You'll constantly be on the hunt for new people to do business with, which will make your life harder. I come from a long and glorious chain of entrepreneurs who lived in scarcity. Everything was harder for them, and they reveled in the difficulty. I don't want to work that hard.

There's a scene in Conan the Barbarian where the master swordsman asks Conan and the other warriors in training, "What is best in life?" The first student says, "Riding on my stallion in the plains with my sword and the wind in my hair." The master says, "No." The second student says, "A fleet of horses at your command." The master says, "No." Then, he says, "Conan! What is best in life?" Conan says, "Crushing your enemies and hearing the lamentation of the women."

That's the scarcity mindset: do or die. That makes sense when you're a warrior fighting for survival, but for most of us, it only leads to misery and, more importantly, stops opportunities from coming your way.

In 2015, I sold an apartment building, made a lot of money, and gave bonuses to everyone who worked there. I thought I was so wildly generous, but one of my investors, Steve, said, "Ben, why didn't you give them bigger bonuses?" I told him, "It's part of your profits. We have more money now because the bonuses came out of the profits from the deal that you invested in." He said, "But you wouldn't have been able to do that deal without these people. You should give them more." I was operating from a scarcity mindset, taking as much as I could for myself and my investors. But Steve taught me an important lesson–I needed to adopt an abundance mindset and be generous to the people who made my success possible.

In my first book, *Born Jumping*, I wrote about the Jumper's Success Formula: intention, discipline, focus, and your code of conduct. These four components are a technique for living a successful life, but now I'm going to argue that they won't do you any good if you apply them without an abundance mindset.

The Jumper's Success Formula:
Intention, Discipline, Focus, and Your Code of Conduct

If you're like Conan the Barbarian, and your intention is to crush your enemy, you could be focused and disciplined and have a code of conduct to get you to this goal, but when you get there, what will you have? If your intention is to make a bunch of money and keep it all for yourself, you could use focus, discipline, and conduct to get there, but when you get there, and you're miserable, what was the point of it all? Being alone sucks. Having a community of people willing to help you feels warm and fuzzy.

Discipline, focus, and intention will get you nowhere if you don't have an abundance mindset. It doesn't do you any good to be focused, disciplined, and intentional about being an angry, lonely jerk.

But an abundance mindset takes you somewhere bigger. An abundance mindset allows you to help more people and bring more love into your life. No one likes the guy who's amazingly disciplined at defeating everyone around him and keeping everything for himself. But when you're the guy who is living in abundance and who wants to bring more to the table for everyone, not just himself, they shower you with roses and throw you a parade. Opportunities abound.

If you are *intentional* about helping others, making the world a better place, and building a community because you're coming from a place of abundance, you could have a life so amazing that you can hardly believe it.

I know because I transformed my life when I shifted from a scarcity mindset to an abundance mindset and pursued my intention to give to charity. It was hard and took a long time. It wasn't my natural way, but I'm so much better for it.

But it was a long journey to get to this point. The work happens on the journey and it's not easy.

High school was the worst time in my life. I had ADHD, so I struggled in class and did not fit in because all the other kids were great students. I was extremely insecure—the chip on my shoulder was so big it made me feel like the Hunchback of Notre Dame.

Simultaneously, I had awesome teachers who taught me the philosophy of living a spiritual life. At the center of that was giving time and money to charity.

The teachers at my high school spoke to us about knowing who we are and where we came from. They taught me that my life is not just about me. I'm a continuation of a chain moving forward through time. I can't live my life just thinking about myself. I had to think bigger. I had a responsibility to contribute to others with what I had instead of just keeping it for myself. This planted the seed of an abundance mindset in me, but I didn't have a clue how to live this way yet.

Trauma is an opportunity that shouldn't go to waste.

I learned later in life that trauma is an opportunity that shouldn't go to waste. You can't change what happened to you in the past, but you can sure as hell change yourself. When I was ten years old, my brother died in a skydiving accident.

My mother became lost in her misery. Three years later, I got shipped off to boarding school, where I did not fit in, and my insecurity grew. For most of my life, I saw my brother's death and my time being sent away to boarding school as the biggest traumatic event of my life. But I would not be the same person I am today if I didn't go through that experience. I also realized years later that my experience at school shaped my beliefs in a positive way, even if I was struggling too much at the time to understand it. My teachers instilled in me the idea of being part of the creation of a better world. Now, I can see my high school experience as a dichotomy: there was frustration and despair, but I also learned to embrace a spiritual life of giving.

I encountered people who showed me unconditional love and kindness. When I was in high school, my friend's family took me skiing three times a year for three years. My family had money. My parents could have paid them back for the ski trips, but they never offered to. I look back on it and realize how thoughtful and kind it was of my friend's family to do that for me. I was so lost and needed that love so much. While my own family was stuck in a scarcity mindset, my friend's family demonstrated abundance.

I got out of high school and went to college, where I majored in weed and girls. I still had a tremendous amount of insecurity, but I covered it up with good looks, an outgoing personality, a six-pack, and a ready smile. But I knew I needed to change, so in my second year of college, I began to consciously work on myself, which included training in martial arts and Taoist philosophy and reading like crazy.

I graduated and went to law school, and when I got out of law school, I was lost. I flunked the bar exam twice, which was humiliating and made me feel like a failure. I knew deep down I didn't want to be a lawyer, but I didn't know what to do with my life. I got a lot of therapy and worked hard at being happy.

At 25, I met my wife, Dorit, and suddenly, I had to grow up and transform from a selfish young badass to a responsible husband who had to make a living and support a family. I had no clue how I was going to pull it off, and I was scared shitless. My first twenty years of marriage were quite challenging, mostly because *I* was in the marriage. I've now been married for thirty-seven years.

In 1988, I got married, moved to Hollywood, Florida, and joined my synagogue. Because I was now a married man, this was the first time in my life that I got formal requests for charity from my religious community.

I was finally able to write checks, so I wrote them. These checks were very small—I was a young man at the beginning of my career, so I wasn't making much money yet. But giving was important to me, so I wrote checks consistently, even if they weren't large. This is where I began with charity, and this is the way most people begin. As time went on, I got more involvement, and my eyes opened to the needs in my community. When my kids went to school, I began to get involved with school boards and learned what it means to be involved in that way.

My eyes opened to the needs in my community.

During that time, I met Howie, who would soon be a mentor, in my synagogue. We eventually were on the board together, and he once told me during a meeting, "Did you have something to say, or did you just want to hear yourself talk?" He helped me learn how to become a good board member and think strategically about getting things done instead of listening to everyone try to sound important in a meeting for four hours.

I started making more money and contributing it to charity, and eventually, I was making and giving enough money that I realized I needed a bigger pond than my synagogue. I got involved with the Jewish Federation in Broward County, Florida, which led me to Jewish Family Services, an organization that does charity work such as feeding the poor and taking the elderly to therapy appointments. From there, my involvement in charities grew as every other part of my life grew.

As my life expanded and my world got bigger, so did my appreciation for the needs of the community. And then, my vision expanded beyond my community, and I became awakened to all the needs in the world.

All around the world, there are people who are hungry. All around the world, there are little old ladies who need people to bring them groceries, bathe them, and clean their houses because they can no longer go down the stairs of their homes. "Nobody will give a shit about these people if I don't," I thought. I can't expect others to care for these people in need because what if no one does? I had to make a contribution.

There's a Rabbinic Parable story about a man who wanted to change the world. He realized he couldn't change the world, so he tried to change his country. He couldn't change his country, so he tried to change his city. He couldn't change his city, so he tried to change his neighborhood. He couldn't change his neighborhood, so he tried to change his family. He couldn't change his family—but he could change himself. The first work has to be done within you, and the work you do to change yourself spirals out and helps others. Only then can you be truly impactful.

I struggled with anger, insecurity, and a scarcity mindset for years, but there were so many people in my life who loved me and were generous to me. I was on the receiving end of so much giving, in so many ways, by so many people, and now I wanted to be the giver and not the recipient. Today, it fills me with such joy to give others the love and kindness that I was given when I was young, scared, and vulnerable.

It took so much more to figure it all out, but I'm finally happy. I'm usually no longer as angry or insecure, and I feel much more complete.

But because I have an abundance mindset, I know it's not enough to have a great life and keep it all to myself. I want to help as many people as possible and share what I have with the world.

Moses could have stayed up on the mountain, reveling in God's spirit. But he didn't. He came down from the mountain, where he was having this tranquil, enlightening experience, to a bunch of whiny people who were complaining because they wanted different food to eat. Yes, we have to seek enlightenment ourselves, we have to be happy, we have to be financially successful, we have to have a beautiful wife who treats us great, and we have to have an abundant table filled with delicious food and wine. But when we have all these things, we can't just stay on the mountaintop (even if our mountaintops are just little hills). We have to come down.

We must share what we've learned and engage with others, even if they're whining and complaining because they haven't reached the top of the mountain yet. We have to come down and deal with reality. Reality is messy. Often, it sucks. It would be easier to just not deal with it, to sit around and drink a nice bottle of wine and enjoy the life I've built. But I know that down the street, there's a poor lady who needs to eat. How could I sit at my table and not help feed her? It's hard, but when you remember that your life isn't just about you, when you remember that you're part of a bigger picture, you realize that you have to join reality and help those that are struggling and suffering.

You don't have to have wealth to give to charity. You can start the process of engaging in charity when you're young and broke. Sure, you may only be able to give $100 when you'll one day be able to give $1 million, but you may still be giving the same percentage of your income.

Honestly, giving that percentage when you're making less money is a bigger gift because you need that money to live. When you're wealthy, it's easy to give because you have excess. When you're not able to give a large sum, it can feel like you're only taking small steps, but giving that percentage is still growth, even if it is only a small amount during a certain time of your life. What matters is getting on the path to becoming charitable.

But to do that, you have to have an abundance mindset. You have to believe that more money will come back to you when you give, and you can't fall into the scarcity mindset trap of holding onto your money because you're scared you won't have enough.

The Hebrew word for love, Ahava, has the root "Hav," meaning "to give." Love is based on giving to the one you care for, and when you give, you receive. In the Biblical Book of Ruth, Naomi and her beautiful daughter-in-law, Ruth, who were both poor widows, move to Bethlehem. Ruth was a Moabite, so the community saw her as an outsider. She regularly harvested leftover grain from the fields of Boaz, a wealthy man. In ancient Israel, this was customary for widows and the poor. When Boaz heard of Ruth's situation, he decided to protect her and let her continue taking more than just the leftover grain from his field. Boaz's charity to Ruth led to their marriage. Not only did Boaz gain a beautiful young wife, but the son they had together became the grandfather of King David. Boaz could have turned away from Ruth and refused to give her anything from his fields, but because he shared his abundance, he was rewarded with a young wife and an amazing future for his family line. That is truly awesome (we should all hope for such rewards in our lives).

CHAPTER 2

Contribution

"Time is more valuable than money. You can get more money, but you cannot get more time."

– Jim Rohn

INFLUENCE

WEALTH

COLLABORATION

RELEVANCE

CONNECTION

CONTRIBUTION

There are four ways to contribute: time, energy, money, and influence.

The way people give money provides a great insight into who they are. It tells you whether someone truly has an abundance mindset or not.

A passage from the Talmud says that a person's character can be discerned in three ways: Kiso (his wallet), Ka'aso (his anger), and Koso (his cup—how he acts when he drinks). How you spend your money reveals who you are—and if you don't give enough to charity, what does that say about you?

When most people want to contribute, the first thing they do is contribute their time by volunteering. Don't get me wrong, we need volunteers... But what if more people knew that you can have a greater impact by writing a check than by spending time volunteering?

Let's consider the example of a food pantry. What does a food pantry need? Money to buy food for the hungry. Sure, they need a team of volunteers to run the pantry, but more than anything, they need money.

If someone is moved to get involved and help this food pantry feed the hungry people of the community, simple math tells us that they could have the greatest impact by writing a check.

The food pantry likely already has a waiting list of volunteers, between teenagers looking to get required volunteer hours for school, retired grandmas looking for a way to get out of the house and make a positive contribution, and countless amazing people in the community who feel called to share their time.

But as a business owner, your time is valuable. If you put a dollar amount to how much you earn per hour of work, your number might be in the hundreds or thousands. Instead of spending your time sweeping the floor of the food pantry, why not spend your time working to close a major deal–and then donate $1 million to the pantry? Your money could help the shelter feed so many more people, and at the end of the day, that's what it's all about.

You can't get any more time than you're given,
but you can always get more money.

In life, you can't get any more time than you're given, but you can always get more money. The food pantry could hire employees to do the work that volunteers do, and you probably earn way more than those employees would. If you make $100 an hour, you could give the soup kitchen that $100, and they could hire 5 people at $20 an hour to serve the food. Doesn't that solve more problems and help more people than standing around serving the food yourself?

If we think about charity like we think about running the business, it's all about the bottom line. Meaning: how many people did you help?

Our goal should be to help as many people as we can, and that goal should guide our decisions about how to contribute. As a wealthy business owner, 99% of the time, your wallet can help more people than your hours of volunteering can. I don't mean to diminish the work of volunteers at all, but there are plenty of people in the world with less wealth who are happy to spend their time volunteering. These people are wonderful, and organizations need them. But if you've been blessed with wealth due to the business you've built, you can help the most people by contributing your wealth. If you're called to volunteer, by all means, volunteer. But if you have wealth, volunteering shouldn't be a substitute for giving money.

When you think about contributing to charity, don't think about what you want to do or what would make you feel good. Think about what's needed.

Let's think about this like a businessperson…

You're probably familiar with the expression, "Work smarter, not harder." If you're running a business, who's more valuable to you: the employee who works very hard but never gets anything done or the employee who doesn't work as hard but gets a tremendous amount done? In business, the amount of effort you put into accomplishing a goal is minor relative to what you accomplish.

If your goal is to feed poor people, volunteering is helpful, but donating money has a bigger impact and requires less effort.

With any charitable contribution you make, ask yourself if what you're doing is truly a good use of your time or if you could have more of an impact writing a check. Forget any excuses you can come up with, and remember all the people in the world who need your money, who could use your money to buy the things they lack.

People think I'm harsh when I say these things, but it's just reality. We want to deal with reality as it is because that's the only way we can improve anything. We can cover it up and gloss over it all we want, but if we want to impact the world, we must face reality. If we can't do that, then what's the point?

I also want to clarify that people who don't have money should absolutely give their time. If all you have to contribute is time, that's amazing. If someone makes $50,000 a year, has two kids, rents an apartment, and didn't grow up in a rich family, and spends Sundays in a homeless shelter, I bow down to them. Given their resources, that's the best way they can contribute. But if someone makes $250,000 a year, grew up wealthy, and owns a nice house, I would implore this person just to write a check.

I also want to clarify that people who don't have money should absolutely give their time. If all you have to contribute is time, that's amazing.

We all have time, but many people are suffering because they don't have enough money. If you have more than enough money, I believe you have an obligation to give some of it away to those who need it.

CHAPTER 3

Connection

"You will get all you want in life if you help enough other people get what they want."

– Zig Ziglar

Who knew that giving to charity was the secret to making people like you more, making your wife nicer to you, and getting invited to better parties?

When you give, one of the first rewards you'll notice is that your relationships become deeper, your life becomes filled with more love, and you'll be able to form meaningful connections with more people. Not only that, but the people you come in contact with will be of much higher quality.

You'll become surrounded by high-quality people—if someone can write huge checks to charity, the odds are that they're successful, ambitious, and interesting…but also generous, abundant, and good-hearted. When you sit on boards or attend donor functions, you'll meet these types of people. Your network will become filled with influential people who have a desire to do good in the world, and when you join forces with them, you can accomplish amazing things. But more importantly, you'll have more friendships in your life, and this is a benefit that's impossible to quantify.

When my daughter got married, I invited over 300 people. Looking around the room at all the incredible people in my life who came to celebrate this moment with my family and me, I realized that I had a wealth of relationships, and many of these relationships would have never come to be without my involvement in charity.

As your wealth and influence grow, you get access to wealthier networks of people who can help you give more to charity, but you may find that some of these people are posers.

I met a guy on a board who wanted to go to lunch with me. I thought he wanted to deepen our relationship, but I didn't realize the truth until I was at the restaurant… He was an insurance guy, and he was working me. He kept asking me financial questions, so I asked them right back. I found out how much he made and how much he gave to charity. At the end of the lunch, I said, "You make a million dollars a year, and you only give $30,000 to charity? Let's just say I responded to him very negatively and aggressively. I'm still a little upset that I reacted the way I did. Oops. My wife thinks I should keep my mouth shut… But I don't want to be friends with people who make lots of money and don't give.

I didn't respond rudely to him just to be a jerk (even if I was…). I want people to wake up and realize that they aren't giving enough. Speaking out about things like this builds a reputation of integrity for givers and the opposite for those who don't give. I want to be the guy who calls out the bullshit, not the guy who sits there and smiles at the board meeting next to people who make a boatload of money and only give a sliver of it to charity. But in order to call out the bullshit and advocate for more wealthy people to give to charity, you have to have wealth and influence and be a peer of the high-net-worth crowd in the first place. You have to earn respect by giving to charity yourself. Otherwise, no one would listen to you.

In short, to have influence, you need a good reputation. And if your reputation is "the guy whose name is on the building because he gave a ton of money to charity," people will treat you with respect.

Reputation is the direct result of relevance. Every day, you're building a reputation, for good or bad, to people who you have no idea might impact your future years down the line.

Maybe you're building a bad reputation and don't even know it. Personally, I feel a moral obligation to share my bad experience with the handful of dishonest business people I've met in my life so I can protect others from being hurt by them. If you do something sleazy or dishonest to one person, I can guarantee that one day, someone you need something from will turn out to be that person's cousin or brother or neighbor, and they'll have heard exactly what you did years ago.

Your reputation is always being made, whether you know it or not. It's better to take action and intentionally build a good reputation by sharing your abundance and deepening your connections with others.

You get influenced by living in abundance and caring about others. The world responds to you based on what you give it.

You put in an input, the world gives you an output. If you touch people in a positive way, you create a sphere of influence…a huge network of people who remember that you touched them in a positive way and are happy to give back to you when they can.

This makes life easier on a simple, everyday level. For example, my Vistage group–a group of CEOs I belong to–was planning a trip, and because I had a personal relationship with the guy planning the trip, I asked him not to plan the trip for dates that I couldn't make. The next year, a different guy was planning the trip, and I had no influence on him because we weren't as close, so I missed that year's trip to Napa Valley.

When my mother passed away, my brothers and I were dividing up her belongings. We put all her jewelry and keepsakes on the dining room table and drew numbers out of a hat to see who would pick first, and then we took turns picking things. At one point, my brother David picked up my grandmother's Shabbat candlesticks. Immediately, I realized I had messed up by not picking those as my first item. "David, I'm sorry, I want those for my daughter," I said. David could have said no. He could have said, "Sure, but trade me that jewelry you already claimed." But he just said, "Here," and gave me the candlesticks.

I'll never forget that moment. David didn't have to give up the candlesticks for me just because I had been an idiot and used my first picks on other things. David performed the relevant act of being generous to me, and for the rest of my life, until I drop dead, my view of David will be influenced by this act. And it had nothing to do with the candlesticks. If those candlesticks were so important to me, I would have taken them in the first 30 choices I had. It had to do with David saying, "Here, give these to your daughter. I love her."

For the rest of my life, until I drop dead, my view of David will be influenced by this act.

Influence doesn't mean transactional. It doesn't mean tit for tat—that I owe David a favor because he did something nice for me. It means that when people are good to each other, they build collaborative relationships where both parties are inclined to help each other out *unconditionally*. If you're keeping a scorecard of your influence over people, you're doing it wrong. When people have true influence with each other, they give from the heart. They don't expect anything in return, but they usually do get something in return because the other person feels happy to give back to them.

It's mutual giving because both people want to, not because they feel they have to. "Scratch my back, and I'll scratch yours," not "Scratch my back so I'm obligated to scratch yours because I'll owe you one." It's, "I've got my hands on these candlesticks, but I see that they're more important to you, so I'm going to release them to you, just as a gift. I don't have to, but I want to. And it makes me happy to release them to you." The relationship reinforces itself because each time someone helps or gives, the other person gets more excited about helping or giving back.

If you're keeping a scorecard of your influence over people, you're doing it wrong.

When you make the transformation to living abundantly and giving away your wealth, your life changes in every arena. Your wife is happier with you because you're now a much nicer person to be around, and you'll have a relationship that is deeper and more full of love than ever before. People like you more, and it's easier to make more friends. Soon, you'll find yourself getting invited to amazing parties with amazing people whom you feel lucky to call your friends and family. You'll deepen your connection to your spirituality and your community. The bottom line: you'll have more love in your life, especially in the way you feel about yourself.

CHAPTER 4

Relevance

"The greatest gift in life is to be remembered."

– Ken Venturi

My brother and I ate breakfast at this little place in Hollywood, Florida. A table of local school teachers sat next to us, and a guy said, "You know who those guys are? Those are the Genets. They are major contributors to the community." I was just eating breakfast in my shorts and t-shirt and thought, "When I die, that's how I want to be remembered." At my Shiva, a 7-day traditional mourning period for Jews where we sit on low chairs and have visitors and communal prayer, I want them to say, "He did well. He made the world better." (They'll probably also say a bunch of negative things that are also true, but that's another story…)

That's relevance: people remember who you are and what you have done. But you can't count on relevance to be permanent. You could give $100,000 to charity, and people could remember it for a day, or they could remember it for decades after you die, and anything in between…

If you're horny or hungry, the next day, you'll be horny and hungry again. Being relevant is like a verb. You're only relevant if you are. It's like running on a treadmill. If you stop, you're no longer relevant. If you don't eat tomorrow, you'll be hungry. If you don't do good works tomorrow, you'll be irrelevant. It took me years to come to terms with that. I actually think it's a good thing now. But it disturbed me for years.

When you stop giving, nobody's going to give a crap about you. They'll think, "What have you done for me lately?" It's like you died, and the world keeps going. Tomorrow, there's still another poor person that needs help. If you don't do it, they'll need to find someone else who will. Influence comes from being on that treadmill, whether it's a pat on the back, your picture in the newspaper, someone wanting to invest with you, or being able to get someone into college.

You can't be relevant yesterday. You're either relevant or irrelevant now. You can send an Ethiopian kid to university and change his whole life, but the feeling you get of being relevant only happens to you that one time. That doesn't mean you didn't change a whole life, but if you want that feeling again tomorrow, you must help someone else. Your work isn't done until your life is over. As a matter of fact, we shouldn't move in any direction that has an end. As I learned from Lee Brower at Strategic Coach, "The enemy of thriving is arriving..."

These days, there are so many people trying to be famous instead of trying to be relevant. Who cares if everyone in the world knows your name because you made a dumb video that went viral? It's much more fulfilling to have 200 people in your local community respect you because you made an impact. You don't need everyone to know who you are and what you've done because it may not be relevant to everyone.

Relevance has nothing to do with self-satisfaction. If you don't appreciate what you did, you're still relevant. If you buy a homeless person dinner or help a single mother pay her rent, you're relevant, whether you bask in that good feeling of helping someone or not. If your actions have a positive effect on the universe, you're relevant.

Being relevant requires action, commitment, and sometimes sacrifice. But if you live the good life and engage the universe in a meaningful way, there are so many beautiful benefits. In so many ways, people see you.

But it's not that I give to charity because I want to be recognized. It's that when I give to charity and I get recognized, I love it. Being recognized isn't the goal, but when it happens, it's awesome.

Being recognized isn't the goal, but when it happens,
it's awesome.

Judah's Story: A Testament to Generosity and Mentorship

I met Judah Hersh when he was just a teenager. He'd been kicked out of his house and was staying with a friend of mine. She'd opened her home to him when he had nowhere else to go, but even the most generous people can't do it all on their own. She told me about his situation, and I decided to help. I wrote a check for $10,000 to cover some of his expenses and make sure he could stay in school. I didn't think much of it at the time—it just felt like the right thing to do. But I had no idea how far that one act of giving would go.

Years later, I was sitting in a restaurant in Boca, and my waiter came over—it was Judah. He's in college, working hard, and trying to figure out his next move. We got to talking, and he said he was interested in real estate. I looked at him and thought, "This kid's got something." So, I made him an offer. I told him, "If you're serious, quit your job and come work for me. But you've got to finish college, no excuses."

He took the offer. Judah came into my office with no experience and no connections, and I'll be honest, the beginning was rough. Real estate isn't easy, and there were days when he wanted to quit. But he stuck it out. I taught him everything I could—how to structure deals, how to manage properties, and how to think big but stay detail-oriented. And, just as important, I showed him that success is about more than making money. It's about building something meaningful.

After a couple of years, he left to start his own thing. I wasn't sure what would happen, but Judah proved me wrong in the best way. He built a successful brokerage, then a private equity firm, and by 2024, we were working together again—this time as partners. In one year, we closed three big deals worth over $18 million.

What really gets me is that Judah didn't even know I was the one who wrote that check all those years ago. He only found out later. That's the beauty of giving—you're not doing it for the credit; you're doing it because it's the right thing to do.

And sometimes, the universe sends it back to you in ways you can't predict.

Judah's story shows exactly what I've been saying throughout this book: generosity creates momentum. You plant a seed, and if the right person picks it up, they'll grow something amazing. Judah didn't just take what I gave him and run—he built a career, a legacy, and a partnership that's brought value to both of us. That's the ripple effect of giving.

When we give, we're not just solving a problem in the moment. We're investing in people to create possibilities. Sometimes, the payoff comes years down the road, and sometimes, it's bigger than you could ever imagine. That's the kind of return on investment you can't put a number on.

That's why I give.

It Feels Good To Give

My wife Dorit and I donated money to build an auditorium for a school in Israel, and we traveled there for the dedication. When we arrived at the school, there were 35 girls waiting at the gate for us, a videographer and photographers, and there was a big sign on the wall that said, "Welcome Ben and Dorit Genet." Our name is on the side of the building.

A leader of the community comes over, gives me a hug, and introduces me to a bunch of people. Then, we started to walk into the school, and all these girls came up to me and my wife and said thank you. We walk into the auditorium, and 300 girls are waiting for us. The music starts, and everyone is clapping. I felt like a movie star, and it was incredibly overwhelming. We listened to presentations, I gave a speech, and my wife sang. And then we went home and went back to normal. But I still reveled in the euphoria of that moment.

Sometimes, however, the pomp and circumstance of external rewards don't fulfill you, and you realize what truly matters.

I received an honorary doctorate from a university for sending amazing Ethiopian students to college. However, at the ceremony, I was frustrated because of some bureaucratic problem with the administration. I was wearing a cap and gown and getting ready to walk into the ceremony and hear all these speeches, and one young Ethiopian man who I'd previously met asked me how I was feeling.

I answered honestly that I was frustrated, and he said, "I don't understand that. You changed our lives. My whole family benefited from what you did. For generations, we will benefit from what you did. How can you feel anything but great?"

This young man's words smacked me upside the head. I realized I'd been stuck in a scarcity mindset, and he knocked me right out of it. It felt like I'd been dipped in a cold spring, and I felt awesome for the rest of the evening. This feeling had nothing to do with influence or any of the other practical, financial benefits of giving. It had to do with the gratifying feeling of self-satisfaction that came from this young man looking me in the eye and telling me that my money had changed his family's life for generations.

There are external benefits to giving to charity, but the most important benefit is the internal feeling you get within yourself. It's the feeling I had when I walked into that auditorium, and the girls were applauding, and the feeling I had when I was a teenager helping kids at a special needs camp. The feeling was the same even though the gifts were on different levels. It's the warm feeling of knowing that you've done something good for someone else. If you've felt any insecurity in life, this feeling helps you fight it.

Many people believe it's selfish to feel good about yourself after you give. It's like the chicken and the egg. Do people give because it makes them feel good? Or do they feel good because they give?

I'm going to argue that it doesn't matter. It's not about the giver—it's about the people being helped. The hungry people in the world don't care why you're giving. They just care that you're giving, and they need more people to give.

The hungry people in the world don't care why you're giving.
They just care that you're giving, and they need more
people to give.

I believe our actions define who we are, and our thoughts are less meaningful. Live a life where you do the right thing. If you're doing the right thing because it makes you feel good, who cares? You're still doing the right thing and helping people who need help.

Real-Life Impact – Oshrit Bekaya

Oshrit Bekaya's story is a good example of what happens when generosity meets ambition. She wasn't asking for help. She was looking for a shot. Through the Ethiopian scholarship program, she got one.

With the scholarship, Oshrit attended a top-tier school in Israel and landed an internship in Miami. That's where things started to shift for her. "The internship made me want to think bigger," she said, "I really want to go big, like they've shown us we can."

Oshrit didn't just gain skills; she gained perspective. She saw that success wasn't just something you achieve for yourself but something you use to help others. "Ben J. gave us a lot of background on himself, his history, and how he became successful," she shared. "It was inspiring to hear his story and see how he used that success to help others."

The scholarship also connected her to the auditorium we built, a space designed to give students more than just a place to sit and learn. "The auditorium isn't just a place for events—it's where people gather, sit, and share ideas," Oshrit said. "It's become a space where we feel like anything is possible."

She's proof that the right kind of help changes everything. Oshrit summed it up best herself: "This whole experience has made me believe in myself and what I can achieve. And someday, I hope to inspire others in the same way."

CHAPTER 5

Collaboration

"Alone we can do so little; together we can do so much."

– Helen Keller

Giving to charity has done more for my business than any marketing strategy could hope to…

As my contributions to charity grew, people realized I was financially successful. They measured my success by the amount I gave. When my donations went from $180 to $1,000 to $1,800 to $3,000 to $5,000, people noticed—and the guy who's giving $5,000 to the synagogue every year must be a good businessman.

People's perceptions of me changed. I got to sit on bigger boards, and the pond that I fished in kept expanding. My relationships with lenders improved. I started getting some investors and making money for other people. My confidence grew, and my insecurity diminished.

My contributions to charity are almost like an advertising campaign. People see my name on the side of the food pantry, or the word gets around that I'm giving thousands to send the children of Ethiopian immigrants in Israel to college, and they think, "Huh, he's clearly doing well." Who do you think they come to the next time they come across a business opportunity?

I walk down the street, and my neighbors don't even say hello. They say, "Do you have a deal?" because they want to invest. You can't write a $500,000 check to charity if you're not making way more than that. So people see you give, and they want to do business with you because they see you're successful.

Giving builds your reputation in two ways: yes, it shows the world that you're good at what you do because you have wealth, but it also shows people that you have an abundant mindset and want to do good in the world. When you have a reputation for giving, people like you more and are more willing to do you favors.

One of the deals that changed my life was a 402-unit apartment building I bought during the recession in 2010. I had no idea that the lawyer representing the seller was married to a woman I knew from my charity work. I was the second highest bidder, and he called me and said, "You're $400,000 below the highest bidder. I'll try to get you this deal as long as you give your word you won't mess with my client." I gave him my word, we got the deal, and owning this building transformed my financial future.

I wasn't even friends with his wife, but she knew my reputation through charity work—and I only found out after the fact that this relationship got me this miraculous deal that put me on the map and got people in my community to take notice of me as a businessman. I made a lot of money for myself and others, and people thought, "Oh, he must know what he's doing," which led to other deals, opportunities, and connections. And it all would have never happened without my contributions to and involvement with charity. In 2010, it wasn't easy to find investors. Outside of my family, my main investors were people I befriended on a charity mission to Ethiopia. It's now thirteen years later, and we have done over ten deals together.

Doing this deal gave me financial confidence, which allowed me to commit $1 million to send Israeli Ethiopians to college. I could have a bigger impact on a cause that was important to me and be a big influence on these students' future due to my business success, which was made possible by my charity work. It's all a circle.

Now, my business is no longer just about making money for me. It's about using my skills in business to earn money for others. The more I earn, the more people's lives I can impact. This fills my career with purpose and energizes me to work. I realized that the real satisfaction of working and being successful doesn't come from the money but from helping other people reach their goals. I feel incredibly fulfilled when I recognize that the smart, driven Ethiopian students I sent to college benefited greatly from my financial help.

Abundance helps you collaborate better with partners, employees, and vendors, both in your business and in the charities you support.

Real-Life Impact: The Dorit and Ben J. Genet Cupboard

One important collaborative relationship I have is with Randy Colman, the President and CEO of Goodman Jewish Family Services of Broward County, the organization that, among many other positive initiatives, runs the Dorit and Ben J. Genet Cupboard.

When Randy described the impact the Cupboard was having on the community, it became clear that we hadn't just started a food pantry—we'd started a movement. "The pantry isn't just about food—it's about relationships, social connection, and the way it's brought our community together," Randy said. That's the kind of ripple effect generosity should have.

Randy broke it down for us: the Cupboard began serving 100 families a month. Today, it serves over 650, providing kosher staples like challah, chicken, and fresh produce to families who need them most. But as Randy pointed out, "It's not just a grocery experience. We've made it a place of dignity, where people feel respected. They choose what they need, just like shopping at any store."

When COVID hit, they didn't stop—they adapted. "People couldn't come in anymore, so we started delivering food," Randy explained. "Now, we have over 100 volunteers every month delivering packages to seniors, Holocaust survivors, and homebound families. It's about more than just the food—it's about showing people they're not alone."

Randy shared one story that stuck with me. "There's a man we call the Avocado Man," he said. "Every time volunteers deliver food to his house, he insists on giving something back. He has an avocado tree and hands them fresh avocados in return. It's his way of showing gratitude."

And then there was the family with disabled children whose van broke down. "We found out the father couldn't get to work or take his kids to doctor appointments. Thanks to donors, we got them a new van. That's what happens when generosity meets need—we solve problems people thought were unsolvable."

The Cupboard also became more than just a Jewish initiative. "Last year, we redistributed nearly a million dollars' worth of non-kosher food to other food banks," Randy shared. "It started as a way to help our community, but now it's helping the broader community, too."

Randy summed it up best: Ben and Dorit didn't just provide seed money—they started something that keeps growing. The pantry has become a lifeline for hundreds of families and a symbol of what happens when generosity is done right."

That's the power of giving. You start with one act, and it turns into a chain reaction of good.

Teen volunteers distribute food to the community at the Dorit and Ben J. Genet Cupboard

When I shifted to abundance, I realized that my previous behavior in business only promoted a one-transaction relationship. You can't do business with someone multiple times if you're busy trying to crush them for every dollar on every deal. When you choose to build collaborative relationships instead, you do better in business, and you feel better about yourself. It's a mindset shift from scarcity to abundance, from transactional to collaborative.

My friend Alan, a broker, brought me a deal. An older gentleman who Alan loved and wanted to protect was selling two buildings, and he sold me one of the deals. I found many problems with the property, and my contract gave me the right to receive financial compensation for these issues. But I wanted to buy his other building, too. So, I kept my mouth shut.

I found similar issues on the next deal we did with this gentleman. I took those $300,000 worth of issues and forced a price reduction. Under the contract terms, I was completely in the right in every way... But this man sold twenty more buildings, and none of them were to me.

I was living in scarcity. I was trying to get every drop of blood out of the stone that I could get. It may have saved me $300,000 at the time, but it cost me tens of millions of dollars in opportunity. These mistakes are what the journey to an abundance mindset is made of. Recognizing this mistake after years of work on self-improvement was the easy part. The work of self-reflection is hard and change is harder, but it is so worth it!

I could have destroyed a relationship with Alan that was very important to me on many levels. We help each other all the time. We collaborate. We care. Without that, I would not have come this far.

When I saved that $300,000, I did a jig, and my partners were high-fiving me, but I didn't realize until later that it was a dumbass move made by a young man who didn't know any better.

My friend Alan, who brought me the deal, was insulted by what I did. He had done a nice thing for me by connecting me to this elderly seller, and I'd gone and smacked the guy upside the head. My contract gave me the right to do that, but my relationship didn't give me the right to do that.

I had to apologize, and over the years, I've acknowledged publicly many times that this was one of the biggest business blunders of my career. This mistake taught me that I couldn't live in scarcity, constantly pinching pennies or trying to squeeze someone for everything they could give me. I had to view deals as partnerships, not competitions.

I have a multi-decades-long friendship with a banker, and we have a symbiotic, collaborative relationship. When I walk into the bank, he trusts me, so the conversation is completely different. We look for ways to benefit each other. It's more profitable for both of our businesses to work in this way, and it feels better to work in collaboration than to try to work each other for every dollar possible.

We never make a vendor wait for their money. We want people to know that we pay our bills on time. They could give us 30 days to pay the bill, but we're not waiting 30 days. If we owe you money, we'll pay you right away. That's abundance—we're not trying to hang on to the money we have as long as possible. We want to pay what we owe.

It's also strategic from a business standpoint. These vendors like me better because I've shown myself to be trustworthy. If one of my buildings needs an air conditioner replaced, a vendor who knows and trusts me is more likely to go the extra mile to get the job done right than a vendor who doesn't trust me because I never pay him on time and won't start work without a large deposit.

I view my investors with a collaborative mindset, too. I help people grow their net worth and their passive monthly income in a hassle-free way so they can achieve financial freedom, and some of them are happy to contribute to what's important to me. My charity work feeds my business, and my business feeds my charity work.

When I lived in a scarcity mindset, I had trouble keeping employees. Now, I have great relationships with my employees— and I have a few that have stayed with me for over a decade. The old me would have driven these people away years ago.

One of my employees, Nancy, has said, "I've never worked for a man who is more willing to work on himself and try to improve constantly." It's gratifying to feel you've earned the respect of those you work with, and you can build incredible relationships with your team when they stay for years. They stop seeing you as the mean, angry boss they can't wait to clock out from every day, and they start to get excited about growing the company.

My employees are passionate about the charity work that I do. They've met the Ethiopian kids that I'm sending to university, and it drives them to work harder and celebrate each deal we make because they see the good that the money we earn does in the world. You begin to feel like a team working toward a common goal rather than a boss telling his underlings what to do so they can collect a paycheck.

I apologize for my deficiencies, and I don't hide my intentions from them. They know that from 9 to 5, our goal is to make money. If somebody doesn't pay us, we have to evict them. But at night, we give some of the money we make to charity. They know where the money we make goes, so the daily pursuit of the dollar turns into a holy enterprise instead of just self-indulgent behavior.

Real Life Impact: Yafit Assien

Generosity has a way of creating something much bigger than its original intention. When we helped build an auditorium at a school in Israel, we didn't just build a structure—we built a space where students could connect, innovate, and feel like they belonged.

"The auditorium has had such a big impact on everyone," Yafit Assien, a student at the school, shared. "It's a place where people can come together for studies, events, and even personal growth."

"It's not just a learning space—it's a place where innovation happens," she said. "It's preparing people for the kinds of challenges that tech and medicine face globally."

For Yafit, the auditorium symbolized more than just a physical space. It represented connection and collaboration—the kind that builds communities. "Seeing the generosity behind the auditorium makes me believe that giving back is something we can all do, in different ways," she said. "It's not just about having a space. It's about what that space allows people to do and the ideas it inspires."

The real impact isn't just in what we built but in how it's being used. Students like Yafit see it as a stepping stone to bigger things. "The impact of a place like this isn't just local," she said. "The students who use it are learning to tackle real-world problems that affect everyone."

Yafit's story reminds me why we give in the first place. It's not about recognition—it's about what happens next. Generosity sparks connection, and connection builds the future.

CHAPTER 6

Wealth

"The only wealth which you will keep forever is the wealth you have given away."

– Marcus Aurelius

There are many ways to be wealthy, and they are created in this order:

1. Wealth of Relationships
2. Monetary Wealth
3. Wealth of Purpose
4. Wealth of Relevance
5. Wealth of Influence

Wealth of Relationships

"Relationships are the foundation of accomplishment."

Early on, before I had any money, I had relationships with people who believed in me and were willing to invest in me both financially and relationally. These relationships led me to financial wealth. I didn't realize that at the time, though. I thought becoming wealthy was just about the money I earned. But in hindsight, I realized I could never have accomplished anything without those relationships. If my mother hadn't trusted and believed in me, she would have never given me the business opportunities that launched my career and led me to my father-in-law. My father-in-law became an influential mentor to whom I owe much of my success.

My friend Howie once told me he loved me, and I said, "You can't love me. You say you love 150 people. You can't love 150 people. You can only really love three or four people." But he said, "I do love 150 people." At the time, I was living in scarcity, and I felt it was impossible for me to love more than three or four people. He taught me that kindness, generosity, and love can be abundant. He taught me how to love people and be nice to people. There I was, 30 years old, and I had to learn how to be nice to people. Until then, I didn't know that was an important part of life. Eventually, I received so much kindness from so many people, and I wanted to be the giver and not only the receiver. From Howie, I learned how to have a true wealth of relationships.

Monetary Wealth

It's very difficult to attain monetary wealth without the wealth of relationships. Nearly every financial opportunity requires someone to know, like, and trust you before they do business with you. The more people you have on your side who believe in you and want to help you succeed, the easier it will be to attain monetary wealth.

Wealth of Purpose

As my financial wealth grew and I could give more to charity, I attained *wealth of purpose*. I began to respect and love myself because I had a clear mission to do good in the world, and I had the financial means to make an impact in cases I cared about. I could let go of the insecurity I had built up as a young man because I saw the good I could do in the world for others, and I grew closer to being at peace.

Wealth of Relevance

When you engage meaningfully with a person or community, you become relevant. You become relevant to the people you help… but also to those who saw or heard about the good you did.

When I was young, I volunteered as a camp counselor at a summer camp in the Catskills for special needs children. One of the highlights was the water fights. They were rowdy, and all the boys loved being a part of them. There was a kid named Cliff who had cerebral palsy and used a wheelchair. During one water fight, he asked my senior counselor, Alan, to get him a cup of water. Alan said, "Get it yourself, Cliff." At first, I thought I had witnessed the meanest thing in the world, and I couldn't believe Alan would be a jerk like that. But when I saw the joy on Cliff's face as he jumped out of his wheelchair and went to get the water on his hands and knees, I understood that Alan wasn't being mean—he was being inspirational. The back of Cliff's hands were bloody from walking on them, but he was smiling with glee. Alan knew that Cliff's parents would never let him experience this. Sure, he could've gotten Cliff the water, but he knew that Cliff would have more fun if he participated himself, even if it was more difficult. Alan was relevant in Cliff's life and mine on that day.

You can become relevant by using your expertise to help others. My friend David is a pediatric surgeon, and one of his greatest satisfactions is helping people find the right doctor. As a business guy, I love to help people get jobs or connect them to the right business opportunities.

When you become relevant, you get external rewards—people see you doing good, and maybe they put your name on a building—but more importantly, you get immense internal rewards. You get to feel the deep satisfaction of knowing you did something good for someone else. When I was in college, I volunteered to teach special needs kids. Looking back, I felt so good contributing to these kids—it was the same level of satisfaction as I would get years later when I was wealthy enough to impact people on a much larger scale. When I was younger, my insecurity overpowered me so that I couldn't revel in these moments of satisfaction, but looking back, I realize my time helping campers was one of the most satisfying moments of my life.

"If you don't remember the past, you can't learn from it."

– Lee Brower

But the thing about relevance is that it's here today and gone tomorrow. People might forget what you did in a month, so you have to help someone else to stay relevant. You can't say, "But remember when I donated $5,000 to the food pantry five years ago?" and expect people to care. Activity begets activity. Stay active, do good in the present, and then you'll be able to enjoy the benefits of being relevant. Relevance is as temporary as life is.

Real-Life Impact—Shani Eshto

Shani Eshto is one of those people who just needed a door
to open. Through the Ethiopian scholarship program, she
got one—and she's making the most of it.

"The internship was an incredible and very professional
experience," Shani said. "It was unique because it wasn't
in my country—it was abroad. That gave me a chance to
see things from an international perspective, which was
really great."

Seeing the world beyond her familiar surroundings gave
her a new way of thinking. She realized education wasn't
just about learning—it was about finding ways to give
back. "This whole experience has inspired me to not only
focus on my education but to educate others about my
heritage," she said. "We do small things now on special
days, but I know this is just the beginning."

Shani's story reminds me why it's worth investing in
people. She's not just taking what she's been given and
using it for herself. She's thinking bigger. "It's starting
small, but it's getting bigger with every step," she said. "For
me, it's impacting not just me but my whole community."

What stood out to me about Shani was how deeply
she connected to the opportunities she'd been given.
She understood that what she'd received came with
responsibility. "Ever since I got back to Israel and back
to school, I thought, 'This is not the end,'" she said. "I
want to experience more, learn more, and apply what I've
learned in practical ways."

That's the whole point of giving—it creates momentum.
When you give to someone like Shani, you're not just

helping her in the moment. You're helping her build something that lasts. She's already thinking about how to inspire others, and how to expand her impact beyond herself. That's the ripple effect we're looking for.

When we help someone like Shani, it's not just her future that changes. It's her community's. And eventually, it's the world's. That's what generosity does—it keeps growing.

Wealth of Influence

When you're relevant over time, you gain influence.

The only way people in my community knew I was starting to do well financially was when they saw how much I gave to charity. I didn't suddenly start driving a fancy car or wearing a flashy watch. But when they saw me write a $5,000 check to charity, they said, "Oh, Genet must be doing well in his business." In a way, it's a marketing tool. More people came to me with business opportunities because they saw my name on a building and assumed I must be successful. I gained influence because I continued to be relevant through my contributions to charity.

There are a million things you do, intentionally or not, that influence the people around you. The bigger your relevance, the more things you touch, and the bigger benefits you get. These benefits could be anything from getting a good parking spot saved for you at a dinner or using your network to help your friend's kid get into college. When you help people, you have their ears. They want to do you favors. This can be a huge advantage in life—and it's exponential. I have personally benefited from the help of those much more influential than I am. I got this help because people deemed me worthy.

The more people you help, the more people are willing to do you favors. You can use these favors to do more good in the world and help more people, and then even more people will have goodwill towards you. More people treat you with kindness or will listen to your opinion.

It's a virtuous cycle.

That's a big deal. When you're at a board meeting, and nobody cares what anyone's saying, but people listen to you because you have influence—that's powerful.

I once wanted a charity I was part of to give $1.5 million to a school. I picked up the phone and called some friends who were past board chairs of the organization, and I asked them to come to the next meeting and speak in favor of the donation. Some of them were investors in my real estate deals. They invested with me because they trusted me, and when the deals were successful, they invested more and liked me more. They were willing to help me because of what I'd done for them and because they believed in the cause. These former board chairs showed up at the meeting and spoke in favor of the donation

I wanted to make to the school. Eighty percent of the board voted with them just because they were influential, and it was a big deal for them to attend a meeting.

There was one important woman on the board who challenged me. I told her that if she gave me her vote, she could count on me to vote for something she cared about one day, and she agreed. I could influence her decision because of my track record of contribution to the organization and my willingness to return the favor. Some people would be offended by this. "It's not fair," they would say. I don't care. We did a lot of good that day, and naysayers are always offended.

It works the same in relationships. My wife is willing to hear me out because she loves and trusts me (It's a good thing she has short-term memory issues and can't remember how much I messed up during our first ten years of marriage!) But because I've built up "love capital," so to speak, she's willing to throw me a bone when I make a mistake.

Influence is earned. If you have deeper relationships with people, they treat you differently than they would treat a transactional party. For example, if you have influence with your employees because they respect you, they'll be more willing to get on board with plans that you propose or go the extra mile at work rather than adopting a transactional "just here to collect my paycheck" mindset.

Asking for what you want is a life skill, but the more influence you have, the faster you get to a yes.

There are times in your life when you can demand things after you have set expectations. And there are times when we can command…

Influence allows you to command respect and get what you want. Of course, you need to learn how to have the courage to ask for it. It's easier to ask when you know the answer will be yes because you have influence in your community and are well respected due to your charitable contributions.

When you get more influence, you can make bigger contributions. When you make bigger contributions, you'll become more relevant. When you become more relevant, you'll be able to be even more influential. The cycle continues in a spiral as your influence expands and your life becomes richer.

CHAPTER 7

Influence

"A life isn't significant except for its impact on other lives."

– Jackie Robinson

Where will you give first?

Too many people get overwhelmed thinking about large-scale issues. But you can help one person or a small group of people, and that has an impact. If you're wondering where to start giving, I recommend looking at your immediate community first. What are the needs in your city, neighborhood, or local religious community? What local organizations could you give to that will make an impact?

When I began my giving journey, I was drawn to Jewish Family Services of Broward County, an organization that provides a range of services to the local Jewish community, including feeding the hungry, taking care of the elderly (some of whom are Holocaust survivors), counseling those in need, supporting survivors of domestic abuse, helping kids in foster care, and more.

I learned that there are around 15,000 members of the Broward County Jewish community facing food insecurity, and 17% of Broward Jewish households live on less than $29,000 a year. As I became more involved in addressing hunger and poverty in my community, I founded the Dorit and Ben J. Genet Cupboard to provide nutritious, kosher food to the hungry in my community. As a matter of fact, one of my friends from the Ethiopian mission, Steve, is the one who asked me for the money for the Cupboard. He was a mentor to me, then a friend, and all the while, an investor. He helped me, I helped him, and together, we helped many people in need.

I quickly realized that giving money was a far more effective way to help the poor in my community than giving my time. People say to me, "Oh, but Ben, I went to the food pantry, and I wanted to volunteer, and they had nothing for me to do." The food pantry needs your money more than it needs your time. Plenty of people are willing to volunteer, but there's a shortage of money to buy food for the poor. It's great that you want to volunteer, but you can make a larger impact by contributing money.

Money solves problems. Yet, for whatever reason, there are usually far more people willing to volunteer than to give money. I think people believe in the fallacy of hard work. They believe that putting in a lot of effort is what makes an impact. The time and effort of volunteers are helpful, but if we're trying to solve the problem of feeding the poor, money will get us closer to our end result.

Contributing money to Jewish Family Services of Broward County and establishing the Cupboard is my way of addressing the needs in my immediate community. But soon, I found I had the financial capacity to give more. I expanded my definition of community to include the Jewish community at large, not just in Broward County. What other needs did my people have that my money could help with?

I began giving to schools in South Florida. But in 2005, after my friend David recommended it, I went to Ethiopia on a charitable mission. Prior to this trip, I had a minimal understanding of the plight of the Ethiopians, but the poverty I saw on this trip was overwhelming. I learned that there were many young Ethiopian Jews who immigrated to Israel and served in the army but came from such poverty that they were unable to get an education when they completed their service.

My brother David funded a scholarship to send one of these students to university. I decided to follow his example and begin funding scholarships as well, and changing their lives in this way has been incredibly moving. Many of their parents were illiterate, and now, because of my gift, these bright young people who grew up in poverty have the opportunity to get an education, pursue their goals, and build a successful future for their families.

I met David, the friend who recommended that I go to Ethiopia, in 1999. He was very involved in charity work, and I admired and respected him. We always said we should do business together.

Years later, in 2019, he called me and said, "Have I got a deal for you." It turned out to be the biggest and best deal of my career… It was a 492,000 sq. ft. small bay warehouse in Tampa, Florida. I knew we had to buy it as soon as I saw it. It was so big that I would have never even looked at it if he didn't call. He was an apartment guy, so he needed my input on a new product type. Once again, it was a win-win. This deal was as transformative as those apartments in 2010. If I weren't involved in charity work, it would have never happened.

My charity work gave me a reputation, influence, and a stronger relationship with my friend. Because of all of those things, he decided I would be his first call when that opportunity came up. We ended up doing seven more deals together. The best part is that these deals, which resulted from my contributions to charity, grew my assets so that I could contribute even more to charity and have an even greater impact on my community.

What is your community—both local and global? What needs are there in the world that you can help solve? When you look at the big picture of needs in the world, it can feel overwhelming. There's so much that needs to be done and so many people who need help every day. But when you zoom in on a specific issue affecting those in your area or in your wider community, it becomes easier to identify how to begin to help.

Remember, you, as one individual, will never be able to save the world. You just need to help where you can, and it will have an impact. It may not feel like much when you help one person, but to one person, that is the world. When we all combine our efforts and take care of our communities, little by little, we can collaborate to make the world a better place.

CHAPTER 8

Thinking Bigger

"Compound interest is the eighth wonder of the world. He who understands it earns it... He who doesn't... pays it."

– Albert Einstein

When you contribute, you gain relevance. When you gain relevance, you gain influence. And when you have influence, you're able to contribute more... And the cycle begins again.

As you spiral up through this virtuous cycle, your ability to impact the world will get bigger and bigger. And when we surround ourselves with like-minded, charitable, engaged people, there is a multiplayer effect, and the results of our charity are compounded. Seek out those people and increase your virtuous, spiraling, intentional power.

Personally, as I've spiraled up through the virtuous cycle, my influence has grown, and I've used it to support political issues related to Israel. I've donated to both sides of the aisle to get people in power to hear what I have to say, and I've had senators over for dinner to discuss the cause. If you'd told my twenty-year-old self, who used to get in trouble with the cops while protesting this same issue, that I'd one day be able to get a United States Senator to sit down and listen to me about Israel, I probably wouldn't have believed you. But this is only possible because of the influence I've built up due to my charity work, and it's now allowing me to have some amount of impact in the political sphere.

Real-Life Impact — Rabbi Brander

When we heard about the impact Rabbi Brander said the auditorium was having, it hit me hard. "The auditorium isn't just a place for performances—it's a sanctuary," he told us. "It allows students and the community to process grief, celebrate life, and find strength in each other."

This wasn't just another building. It became a lifeline for students and families dealing with unimaginable pain. Rabbi Brander talked about what happens in Gush Etzion—a place where life is fragile and tragedy can strike without warning. "Students lose classmates to terror attacks. Teachers are injured. Entire families are torn apart," he said. "We didn't have a place for them to come together and process that kind of loss until now."

The auditorium changed that. It gave them a space to gather, to heal, and to rediscover hope. "After the Nova Festival tragedy, where so many were killed and injured, students came here and had the courage to sing and dance again," Rabbi Brander shared. "Their message was clear: we will not let our enemies destroy our ability to create, to celebrate, and to hope."

It's not just about mourning, either. This space has become a beacon for the entire region. "The auditorium radiates good energy," Rabbi Brander said. "It's more than a safe space—it's a place where students can find their music, their voice, and their potential."

Rabbi Brander told us about one of the guidance counselors at the school, a woman who lost her own daughter to violence. "Even she uses this space to help others heal," he said. "It's where mourning coexists with hope, where creating music or art becomes an act of defiance against despair."

This is what happens when we give with intention. We didn't just build a building. We created a space where people could heal and grow. We gave them a reason to keep going.

Rabbi Brander summed it up best: "This space is holy. It's more than bricks and mortar. It's where the best of humanity is fostered, even in one of the most challenging regions of the world."

That's the kind of impact generosity can have. You build a space, and you give people the tools to fill it with hope, resilience, and meaning. I believe that's how you change the world.

With your influence, you'll build a reputation, and that reputation will be like a currency that helps you accomplish what you want to accomplish.

Someone came to me for help getting his son into university because he'd had trouble in school and gotten kicked out of high school. I called this school that I've sent all these Ethiopian students to and said, "Here's a good kid; he's gotten into some trouble, but he's a solid kid. Interview him, and see if you can take him into your one-year international program." He got in, and he was then able to transfer to college, even without a high school degree, because he had one year of a college transcript. Little old me was able to have a real impact on someone's life. I wouldn't have been able to do that if I hadn't given this school $200,000 a year for five years and built up a good reputation with its administrators.

Most of the time, we're not aware of our reputational value. People with bad reputations don't know the price they're paying regularly, and people with good reputations don't realize that all the blessings in their lives result from their good reputations. Each day, we take actions, whether they're good or bad, and these actions build our reputation. You may not find out until ten years later that an action you took changed the course of your life because it changed how one person saw you.

"The difference between doing nothing and the 1st step is infinite."

I decided to use my influence to become a vocal advocate for charity. When I tell people that I plan to give a million dollars to charity this year, they look at me like I'm bragging. But I'm not ashamed. I'm going to put my name on a building, an ambulance, a school. I want people to see that I'm doing charity so I can engage them to give charity, too. If people tell me their parents always gave anonymously, I say, "Oh, that's nice." But what I don't say is that many people use anonymity to hide.

The anonymous thing gives people an excuse not to give at all or to give less than they could. People think that it's bragging to give large sums of money or to talk about giving to charity, so some sit on their asses and don't give anything at all. But I decided to be vocal about giving to charity because that's the best way I know to get more people to realize how important it is. The hungry kids of the world don't care if the person who feeds them made an anonymous donation or not.

Also, let's be real. There are just a few people in the world who are truly altruistic, give large sums of money, and remain anonymous. But most of us aren't that pure of heart.

People insult you for wanting to put your name on a building, but my response is, "Okay, go write a check." I'm a marketing guy. I believe that being vocal about your charity is a way to influence others to do the same.

I have no intention to hide the fact that I intend to give away half my net worth in my lifetime. I intend to wake people up to the possibility of doing the same thing because the rewards are enormous, and there are so many needs in the world to take care of.

And when I advocate for charity, I'm not saying you need to give to the same causes I give to. Give to what's important to you and what moves you to give. So many problems in the world could be solved with money. If I give to what moves me and you give to what moves you, we'll cover a lot of bases.

There's a swirling, all-powerful energy source of the universe that I call God. Everything you do can affect everything that's part of this energy source of the universe. Now, you can't control everything—shit happens. You could still get cancer or get into a car accident tomorrow. That's just life. But what you put out into this energy of the universe can have massive benefits.

It's like having a tree in your backyard. If you fertilize your tree every day, it will produce more fruit than your neighbor who ignores his tree. You can fertilize your relationships by helping people, and these relationships will bear fruit. We may not even realize that the good things in our lives result from the people we've helped.

Let's say you close a big deal, but you have no idea that a week ago, the other party was talking to someone of influence and said, "I want to do business with this guy. What do you think of him?" and the person said, "He's an honorable, charitable man" because he's seen the charity work you do.

You get an amazing feeling when you give, whether it's money, making a call and using your influence to help someone, or spending time with someone who needs love. You take something valuable, you freely give it, and every time you do that, you feel good.

Just jump and do something; it doesn't matter what it is, and it will change you and create some impact. Action begets action. Stagnation begets stagnation. An object in motion tends to stay in motion. Jump in and give, and watch your life grow richer.

Real-Life Impact – Gal Gwangool

Gal Gwangool didn't know what to expect when he joined the Miami internship program. "I knew Ben J. donated to our university, but I didn't know what else he does," Gal shared. "Now, after seeing everything, it makes me think about what I could do someday—like raising donations or starting something of my own."

The internship wasn't just a chance to learn practical skills. It gave Gal a new way of thinking about success and the role generosity plays in it. Gal also saw firsthand what it means to turn success into something meaningful. "Ben J. always told us that success is more than personal—it's about using what you've achieved to make a difference for others. Seeing that in action was eye-opening."

During his time in Miami, Gal began to see how generosity creates ripple effects that go far beyond the initial act. "It's not just about giving to solve a problem. It's about showing people what's possible, so they start thinking about how they can give, too," he said. "That's what stuck with me. It made me realize that one person's generosity can inspire a whole chain of impact."

Gal's story is proof that giving doesn't just help the person receiving it—it transforms them. He left Miami not only with new skills but with a roadmap for the future. "I thought I knew what success looked like before," Gal said. "But now, I see it differently. It's about making a difference, not just for yourself but for the people around you."

That's the point of giving. When you create opportunities for others, you're not just solving today's problems—you're building tomorrow's leaders.

CONCLUSION

Through charity work that I'm involved in, I met and became friends with a young guy named Jarred. He called me one day and said, "I found this deal, Ben J., I'm not sure what to do with it."

I said, "I'll meet you at the property in an hour." I was much more senior and experienced in real estate, so I knew Jarred needed my advice. I drove to the property, looked at it, and said, "You have to buy this deal. Don't think, just buy it. It's an amazing deal. If you don't buy it, I'll buy it. But you need to buy it."

Thanks to the boost of confidence I gave him, Jarred bought the deal, which brought him success. He was appreciative of my help, and we became better friends.

A few years later, he called me and said, "I've found this 202,000-square-foot industrial deal in Tampa. Do you want to do the deal with me?" We drove up to Tampa, and after looking at the property for thirty seconds, I knew I wanted to own it.

We went to buy it together, and the seller wouldn't come down to our price.

Jarred was going to walk over $500,000, so I said, "I'll take the whole thing, and I'll pay the $500,000 if you don't want it." We paid the additional money, we got the deal, and we own it today. It was an amazing deal, and it was the first deal I ever did north of my territory. It opened me up to so many opportunities. Since then, we've done a total of four deals together. I made millions of dollars, and it all came as a result of my engagement in charity directly and my kindness to him and his reciprocation.

We were at a charity event, and Jarred spoke on a panel. He looked out into the audience at me and spoke about what I did for him and my charity work. After the panel, we were standing by the bar, and a man came up to us and started talking. He told me he was one of the bidders on my buildings. We struck up a friendship, began having lunch together, and planned to do business together when the right opportunity came along.

Recently, after a large deal, I went to a charity event to rebuild a Jewish community center that was burned by an anti-Semitic piece of crap. I was sitting with one of my investors, who is one of the wealthiest guys I know, and I told him, "You're going to make half a million dollars tomorrow…" Another wealthy guy who was standing nearby overheard us talking and said, "How come I'm not in the deal?" We started talking, and by the end of the conversation, this wealthy guy was interested in investing in my future deals. I scored a major investor, and it wasn't because of any fancy marketing strategy or business plan... It was because I donated money to rebuild the community center and ended up at a charity event with a bunch of successful and charitable guys.

Now, I didn't go to the charity event to network with rich guys. I went because I wanted to help rebuild the community center. But the more I give to charity, the more I find myself in "lucky" situations that enable me to make more money, which enables me to give more money to charity... And the cycle continues...

These are small examples of the chain reaction that happens when you engage with others. Remember the Kung Fu master moving in a swirling motion, building momentum until–BAM!--he punches with a big impact. Or the tornado that swirls and swirls, accumulating power until it touches the ground with force.

Or think of it as an investment that compounds for years. You will receive massive dividends in contribution (impact), wealth, connection and collaboration (relationships), and relevance (influence) from what you've contributed over time.

Each time I do something good for others, it begins a chain reaction that brings good back into my life. I may not see the benefit until years later, but the momentum I build today will help me tomorrow. Engagement, helping others, and giving to charity all feed into this cycle that builds momentum and adds value to my life…and will add value for generations to come. When and if my kids come into my business, I know that there's a huge network of people who have goodwill towards me and will be excited to help my kids. The circle of influence will continue to grow.

And the impact goes way beyond business opportunities or new friends. When your swirling momentum grows, it'll be there for you in the hardest moments of your life. My son had a brain bleed and needed brain surgery. After the MRI, my wife and I were sitting at home, crying, overwhelmed, and not sure what to do. But several friends came over, sat with us for many hours, pored over the medical documents, got on the phone with doctors, and helped us decide what to do. It had a major impact on our son's life… But having these friends willing to be there for us was no accident. It was the profit of deep relationships.

If you don't prepare in advance, when you need help, it won't appear. But when you engage in meaningful activity and build your swirls of momentum, help will be there when you need it. But you can't wait until you need it to go get it.

The best part of building my swirls of momentum is that helping others and giving to charity is pleasurable to me. I enjoy doing these things–it's fun. But even if it isn't pleasurable to you, it's an activity you need to do because it makes your life better. It's like exercise. Some people love to go to the gym, and some people hate it, but if you want to live a healthy life, you must do it, like it or not.

Engaging in meaningful activity, whether you like it or not, will help you succeed. But it's better to choose to like it... It's better to choose to be happy than to choose to be miserable. "You get to, not got to!"

Everything in life is a choice, and it's not always easy to choose. Staying home and watching Netflix is easier than attending a boring charity meeting. But when you park your car for a boring charity meeting, you might have a nice conversation with someone in the parking lot. Ten years later, that conversation leads to an opportunity that changes your life.

Action begets action, and every action has an equal and opposite reaction. These are the laws of the universe. If you intentionally apply these laws of the universe to your future, your success will be greatly enhanced. I would have been successful no matter what, but not like this.

During the course of editing this book, the war in Israel began. I've been politically involved in both the United States and Israel, but when this war started, I felt useless and insufficient. I felt as though all the work I'd done had been meaningless, and any sense of control over my surroundings disappeared. "What can I do now?" I thought. But after a flood comes a rebirth.

I decided it was time to double down, focus, get more involved, and put my money where my mouth is. I decided to reallocate my time and money to what was most important to me. When things are going well, your vision gets blurred. But when a tragedy like this hits you out of nowhere, it makes you laser-focus on what is crucial in your life. Personally, I plan to travel to Israel and do manual labor—since everyone is at war, there's a shortage of people to work. I'm still going to write big-ass checks, but it's important to me to also be there in person to offer what help I can.

But I need to recognize that going to volunteer is for me. It's so that I can feel like I'm contributing to something I care about and stop feeling so useless. An Israeli woman whose house got blown up and whose family members have been killed isn't going to be helped much by my manual labor. What she needs is a check to rebuild her house. Volunteering is great, but it doesn't replace the need to give money. My volunteering is an addition to the monetary contributions I've already made. As long as you keep in mind that the people you're helping need your money more than your time, by all means, volunteer for a cause you care about so you can experience the rewarding feeling of being part of something greater than yourself.

Recently, I was on a friend's private jet flying to DC. I was sitting across from a rabbi. Now, I have no interest in meeting a new rabbi. I already know a million rabbis, and they all want my money. I'm happy to give, but I'm not exactly taking applications for new rabbis. However, this rabbi told me a story:

He went to see one of his congregants, who was a doctor and brought him Matzah on Passover. A lady was sitting in the waiting room, and the rabbi asked if she was Jewish. She said yes, and he offered her a box of Matzah. She started screaming at him: "How dare you give me this! How dare you assume I want this!" After she yelled at him, he gave her his business card and told her she could call if she needed anything.

Six years later, the rabbi gets a call. The voice on the phone says, "Do you remember me? I'm the lady who was rude to you about the matzah in the doctor's office." The rabbi said, "Of course I remember." "My father is 72 years old. They gave him two days to live, and he wants to meet a rabbi."

The rabbi goes to meet her father and spends time with him during the final days of his life. The rabbi tells the man that he's a righteous person and consoles him as he prepares to die.

The father asked for a Jewish funeral, so the rabbi arranged it. The cost of the funeral was $6,500, and the daughter wrote the rabbi a check for $592, which was just the cost of cremation. This was a wealthy family... But the daughter didn't care that her father wanted a Jewish funeral, so she only wanted to pay for the cremation. The rabbi ended up doing charity for the rich and collected the money to give the father a Jewish funeral.

About eight years later, the rabbi is doing a program at his temple about feeding the poor and helping people. Again, the woman turns up and says, "I hope you remember me. I'm the lady who yelled about the Matzah. You spent time with my father when he died. Here's a check for $10,000. I appreciate the good you're doing."

When I heard the story, my first instinct was, "Personally, it's not worth the ten grand... Who does this lady think she is?"

But the rabbi told me, "You have to believe in the good of a person's soul. It might take them 25 years to bring it out, but you must be softer and more appreciative."

That was the message I needed to hear.

I know how to write a check to charity. But I sure as hell need to be more open to people who are flawed and try to see the good in every person's soul.

Funny how this epiphany started with me thinking, "Oh, great, I'm stuck talking to another rabbi." I didn't even want to spend my flight talking to this guy, but he taught me a meaningful lesson that I needed to hear.

I told this story in the book because I don't want anyone to get the impression that just because I wrote a book about charity, I think I'm some guy who has all the answers. I have my flaws like anyone, and I need to grow where I need to grow. It's not easy to make a change, but I'm working on it.

I hope this book has challenged your thinking about charity and opened the door for you to transform your life and impact the world through giving. Get out there, give, and watch your virtuous cycle grow bigger and bigger.

ABOUT THE AUTHOR

Benjamin Genet began his career in real estate in 1988 and over a 37-year span he has successfully owned and managed over 67 Commercial and Residential properties. He remains active and engaged as President of his management company, Genet Property Group. He resides in South Florida with his wife of 37 years, Dorit, and together they are the proud parents of three wonderful children, a great son-in-law and two grandchildren.

www.ingramcontent.com/pod-product-compliance
Lightning Source LLC
Chambersburg PA
CBHW071515200326
41519CB00019B/5946